VOICES OF YOUNG HEROES

LET'S GO GET 'EM!

U.S. MARINES

Beck Engraving Co., Phila., Pa., Reqn.—469-1943, 7-11-42, 50M.

HISTORY SPEAKS!

VOICES OF YOUNG HEROES

A WORLD WAR II BOOK FOR KIDS

KELLY MILNER HALLS

ROCKRIDGE
PRESS

Interior and Cover Designer: John Clifford
Art Producer: Hannah Dickerson
Editor: Eliza Kirby
Production Editor: Jenna Dutton

Alamy Stock Photo/Aero Archive, cover (left) and pp. 10, 64; Alamy Stock Photo/dpa picture alliance, cover (background), interior borders and pp. 11, 26; Shutterstock/Ivan Cholakov, cover (center); Alamy Stock Photo/Photo 12, cover (right) and p. 90; Shutterstock/Everett Historical, pp. ii, 3, 44, 78, 84, 85, 89; Alamy Stock Photo/American Photo Archive, p. 4; Creative Market/Semicircular, pp. 8-9; Getty Images/Keystone Features, p. 14; Shutterstock/ Kyle Lee, p. 16; Alamy Stock Photo/Lordprice Collection, p. 19; Wikimedia Commons/ Hinnerk11/CC BY-SA (https://creativecommons.org/licenses/by-sa/4.0), p. 21; Bridgeman Images/British Library Board, p. 22; Library of Congress, Prints & Photographs Division, Bain News Service collection, LC-DIG-ggbain-18600, p. 25; Shutterstock/anahtiris, p. 27; Wikimedia Commons/German Government/Public domain, p. 30; Alamy Stock Photo/History and Art Collection, p. 33; Alamy Stock Photo/Bruno Coelho, p. 35; Alamy Stock Photo/ timsimages, p. 36; Courtesy of the National Hannie Schaft Foundation, p. 39; Library of Congress, Prints & Photographs Division, Photochrom Print Collection/Detroit Publishing Company, LC-DIG-ppmsc-05818, p. 40; U.S. Naval History and Heritage Command Photograph, Collection of Fleet Admiral Chester W. Nimitz, USN., p. 43; Alamy Stock Photo/ Historic Images, p. 48; Alamy Stock Photo/Ryhor Bruyeu, p. 49; Alamy Stock Photo/Bill Bachmann, p. 53; iStock/Gelia, p. 54; Alamy Stock Photo/Gibson Green, p. 56; Alamy Stock Photo/Niday Picture Library, pp. 57, 72; Creative Commons/Churchill Club/CC BY-SA (CC BY-SA 4.0), p. 61; Alamy Stock Photo/World History Archive, pp. 62, 74; iStock/Joesboy, p. 67; Shutterstock/bissig, p. 70; Shutterstock/Sytilin Pavel, p. 71; Alamy Stock Photo/Military Images, p. 77; Alamy Stock Photo/akg-images, p. 81; Alamy Stock Photo/The Print Collector, p. 82. Author photo courtesy of Roxyanne Young.

ISBN: Print 978-1-64611-421-4 | eBook 978-1-64611-422-1

R0

CONTENTS

INTRODUCTION

World War II (1939–1945) was the deadliest, most far-reaching war in global history. It was a war of good versus evil—a war of the Allied Powers versus the Axis Powers.

The Allied nations were the United States, Great Britain, France, Russia, and China, although all of the United Nations opposed the Axis invasions. The Axis nations were Germany, Italy, and Japan; however, Spain and Russia had short relationships with the Axis, too.

Because the Allies had more countries on their side, they might have seemed far stronger than the Axis Powers, but they were not as quick to do battle as the Axis Powers. By the time they combined their military might, the Axis Powers had already occupied a huge part of Europe, Russia, Asia, and the Middle East.

Adolf Hitler, of **Nazi** Germany, is the best-known Axis leader, but he was not alone. Italian dictator Benito Mussolini had taken control of Italy in 1922, more than a decade before Hitler gained power in Germany in 1933. Hirohito was the third Axis leader. He had been crowned the emperor of Japan in 1926.

When people from all walks of life go to war, lives are lost. More than 75 million people died in World War II. The loss is painful for all of the soldiers' families, no matter which side they are on. But they are not the only casualties of war. Children are affected by the violence, too.

Children often do all they can to help push their nations to victory. When they cannot help, they fight for something far more basic than winning. They fight simply to survive. This book will introduce you to 22 young people from the time of World War II and show you how the war colored their lives.

You'll get to know famous heroes, like Jewish teenager Anne Frank, who didn't survive the war but inspired generations to come with her moving, true-life diary passages about it. You'll meet lesser-known heroes, like 12-year-old United States soldier Calvin Graham, who lied about his age so he could fight for justice in Europe. You'll even read about Helmuth Hübener, a young German boy who recognized Hitler's evil and gave his life to help stop it.

As you read their stories, you'll begin to understand how war affects children worldwide. And perhaps you'll recognize how learning about the past can protect us in the future, assuming we learn the lessons that war has to teach us. You may even see the power each of us has to do good at any age.

As you read, you may come upon words you don't understand. Check the Glossary in the back to help you learn. If you are eager to know more about World War II, the Resources section offers great books, museums, and websites you can explore.

If we study the worst war in human history, if we understand how war hurts everyone, we might be able to stop it from happening again.

WORLD WAR II

World War II, also known as the Second World War, was a worldwide war that began in 1939 and ended in 1945. It involved more than 30 countries. Not only did many soldiers die in the war, but Adolf Hitler's government caused the deaths of millions of Jewish people.

WHY IT HAPPENED

When World War I ended on November 11, 1918, people around the world were relieved. More than 20 million people had been lost to global violence, and just as many had been wounded but survived.

Germany was blamed for most of the death and destruction. Borders were redrawn, treaties were signed, and punishment was doled out. The German government was ordered to make restitution. They would pay France and Great Britain £6.6 billion (pounds), or more than $400 billion in today's money, for the damage caused.

The problem was that Germany had no way to raise that much money, even if they were to blame. What was left of their postwar economy soon crumbled. Unemployment skyrocketed, and the German people lived in poverty.

A powerful politician and war veteran named Adolf Hitler claimed to have the answers that would save their country. He led a new party called the National Socialist German Workers' Party, or Nazi Party, and was named chancellor, head of the German nation, in January 1933.

Though Germany was not allowed to have a large army or navy, and no air force at all, after World War I, Hitler expanded his nation's technology and military strength—in secret at first, then openly. Slowly but surely, his forces began to reclaim territory that had previously been under German control.

Most nations were tired of war. They couldn't stomach another fight, so they let Germany absorb a number of smaller countries without opposition. By the time they realized Hitler dreamt of world domination, it was too late. A war between good and evil had begun. Germany, Italy, and Japan wanted power. The rest of the world wanted freedom. So the fighting began.

WHO WAS INVOLVED

The Axis Powers squared off against the Allied Powers. But who was on each side of the battle?

As mentioned, the Allied nations were the United States of America, Great Britain, France, Russia, and China. The Axis nations were Germany, Italy, and Japan, with some assistance from Spain. Their leaders were as diverse then as they are now.

Adolf Hitler, the leader of Germany and later known as the Führer, wanted to transform his country into what he called a "pure" nation—a country that welcomed only healthy, able-bodied, heterosexual white

German police marching in Austria

citizens. He was prepared, and even eager, to remove every Jewish, Romany, disabled, or gay person from his country. But he wasn't content only to force them to move away. He was ready to kill them for even the smallest of crimes.

Hitler also sent millions of Jewish people to work camps, where they labored without decent food, clothing, housing, or rest. Once all their energy was gone, many of the workers died in Hitler's service. As bad as that was, it wasn't Hitler's greatest crime against Jewish people. His worst evil came when he ordered millions of Jews to die in poisonous gas chambers.

The explosion of the USS *Shaw*, an American naval ship, during the Japanese attack on Pearl Harbor

Benito Mussolini, a dictator ruling Italy, agreed with Hitler's deadly ideology and signed a treaty promising that his country would fight alongside Germany. Hirohito, emperor of the Japanese Empire, joined Germany and Italy in their deadly advances.

Neville Chamberlain, prime minister of Great Britain, saw Hitler as no real threat at first, but he soon changed his mind as the German leader took over European country after European country. Chamberlain understood that his country could be next, so together with the leader of France, he called for a war against Germany on September 3, 1939. Winston Churchill was elected in 1940 and served as prime minister for the rest of the war.

American president Franklin Delano Roosevelt was slower to get involved. He was trying to help the United States recover from World War I and the Great Depression, an economic collapse that left millions of Americans penniless. So he chose to be neutral—until Japan bombed Pearl Harbor in Hawaii on December 7, 1941. So many lives were lost, and so many ships and aircraft were destroyed, that Roosevelt knew he had no choice. He joined the Allied Powers.

Joseph Stalin, the Communist dictator of the Soviet Union, which is now known as Russia, took both sides. At first, he signed a nonaggression treaty with Germany in 1939. But when Hitler double-crossed him and invaded the Soviet Union in 1941, Stalin switched sides and stood with the Allied Powers until Hitler was defeated.

Though China receives little credit for its efforts during World War II, the country was the first and poorest of the Allied Powers to take on the Axis Powers, in 1937. Chiang Kai-shek led the Chinese Nationalist forces, and Mao Zedong led the Communist resistance.

THE MAJOR EVENTS AND THE OUTCOME

For six years, the Axis forces tried to take over the world, capturing territory in Europe, Russia, Asia, and the Middle East by force. Five of the worst battles in human history unfolded during World War II.

The Holocaust, one of the most awful things to ever happen, also occurred during this time. More than six million Jewish people were killed by the Nazis. Between 1933 and 1945, Hitler and the Nazis wiped out about two-thirds of Europe's Jewish population. Hitler also ordered the Nazis to kill other people that he didn't like. Polish people, Catholics, Serbs, Africans, gay men, and disabled people were rounded up. By some counts, the Nazis murdered as many as 20 million innocent people

It's almost impossible to imagine the total loss of life during World War II. Because three power-greedy dictators wanted to rule the world, 75 million lives were lost. While every life sacrificed was important, eight countries lost one million citizens or more. Soldiers died by way of bullets and bombs, rockets and shrapnel. Civilians died by the same wartime means, with starvation, sickness, atomic bombs, and purposeful extermination thrown into the mix.

Survivors said, "Never again," and promised to remember those lost. They set out to prevent such a war from ever happening again. And yet world leaders sometimes ignore the mistakes of history and repeat them in the future.

Your generation does not have to make the same mistakes. As you read the stories of children during World War II, you might move toward a greater destiny, one that will guarantee that the promise of "Never again" will be kept.

WORLD WAR II

Began **1939**	Ended **1945**

United States
420,000
lives lost

Allied Countries

Axis Countries

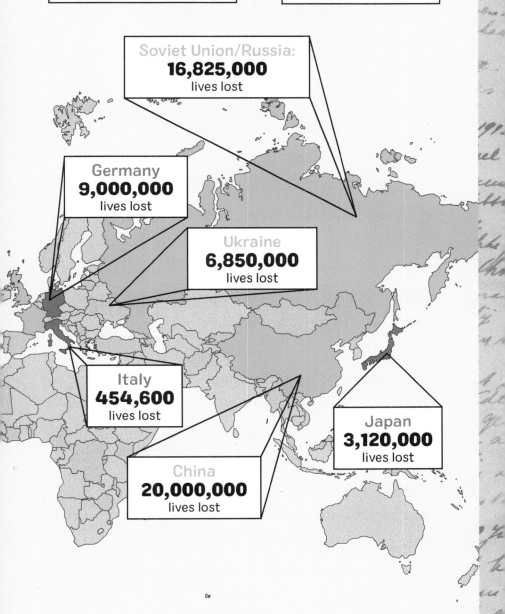

Number of soldiers
who fought:
70 million

Number of
lives lost:
75 million

Soviet Union/Russia:
16,825,000
lives lost

Germany
9,000,000
lives lost

Ukraine
6,850,000
lives lost

Italy
454,600
lives lost

China
20,000,000
lives lost

Japan
3,120,000
lives lost

Anne Frank

Anne Frank was born on June 12, 1929, in Frankfurt, Germany, the daughter of Jewish banker Otto Frank and his wife, Edith. Anne, her parents, and her older sister, Margot, lived happily until Adolf Hitler took control of their country in 1933.

Hitler was the newly elected leader of Germany and the head of the Nazi Party. He envisioned a Germany made up of a white population he called the Aryan race, which he considered to be superior. And he saw no place for people he considered inferior, including the Jews.

Those who resisted Hitler's vision were silenced, arrested, or killed. Books that didn't support his ideals were burned. So Otto Frank moved his family to Amsterdam, in the Netherlands, to keep them safe.

Happiness in the Frank family was restored, but it didn't last. On May 10, 1940, the Nazis invaded the Netherlands. Jewish people were forced to carry special papers that showed their heritage. They were even marked with bright yellow stars on their clothing.

On her 13th birthday, Anne was gifted a diary with a red plaid cover. "I hope I will be able to confide everything to you," she wrote in her first entry, "as I have never been able to confide in anyone."

One month later, Anne's sister was ordered to report to a work camp in Germany—a death camp for Jews. To escape the deadly order, the Franks went into hiding. The building where Otto worked had an annex above the factory. Trusted

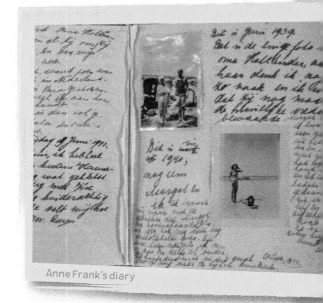

Anne Frank's diary

coworkers built a bookshelf on a hinge—a secret door to protect the Franks from discovery.

They claimed two rooms on the second floor. The rooms were small and dark and had almost no furniture. The windows were covered with paper so that nobody could see them hiding inside. Anne and Margot's room felt lonely and sad, so Anne scattered pictures across the walls to lighten the mood.

> **"IT'S A WONDER I HAVEN'T ABANDONED ALL MY IDEALS . . . YET I CLING TO THEM BECAUSE I STILL BELIEVE, IN SPITE OF EVERYTHING, THAT PEOPLE ARE TRULY GOOD AT HEART."**
> —Anne Frank

The Van Pels family—Hermann, Auguste, and their son, Peter—moved into two rooms on the floor above them. Otto Frank's work friends provided supplies when it was safe. When Fritz Pfeffer arrived in November, Anne was forced to share her room. His stories of Jews packed into railroad cattle cars and gas chambers frightened her, but she clung to hope.

For two years, the eight people above the factory kept silent all day to escape detection. At night, when the workers left, the radio softly played, giving reports on the war. The Allies were gaining on Hitler's armies. It was thought that the war might be over soon, and the families in hiding learned that a search was on for true war stories to document its history.

Anne began to revise her diaries for publication. She and Margot dreamt of going back to school. But their dreams were shattered. On August 4, 1944, Nazi police officers known as the Gestapo stormed the factory, thanks to an anonymous tip. All eight refugees were arrested.

Anne and Margot wound up at Bergen-Belsen, a concentration camp in Germany. Margot died of typhus in March 1945. Anne passed away a few days later. Only Otto Frank survived to see the end of World War II. He published Anne's writings, fulfilling her last wish.

DID YOU KNOW?

More than 30 million copies of *The Diary of Anne Frank* have been sold, and it's been translated into 70 different languages, proving that although Anne Frank is gone, she is not forgotten.

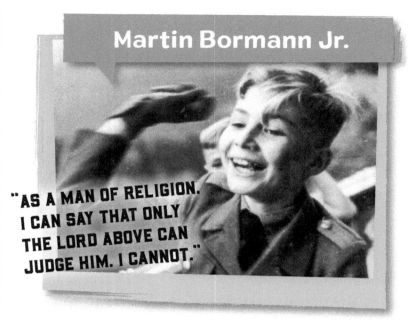

Martin Bormann Jr.

"AS A MAN OF RELIGION, I CAN SAY THAT ONLY THE LORD ABOVE CAN JUDGE HIM. I CANNOT."

Martin Bormann Jr. was the first of 10 children born in Grunwald, Bavaria, to Martin and Gerda Bormann. Born April 14, 1930, he was like any other child, with one exception. His nickname was "Kronzi," the German word for "crown prince." And he was Adolf Hitler's first godson.

Martin Bormann Sr. was the Führer's communications secretary and second in German command. He handled Hitler's schedule and appointment calendar. He controlled German legislation, and he enthusiastically encouraged the extermination of Jews and other people Hitler considered inferior.

Martin Jr. knew nothing of his father's war crimes. In fact, he had no concept of Nazi evil until he was in his mid-teens. As a little boy, he saw his father as a strict man, but a good father who had grown up in poverty and wanted a better life for his 10 children. Work kept him away for months at a time, but his family was wealthy, happy, and safe.

Martin Jr. saw Hitler a little differently. Hitler seemed uneasy when he visited their home in Obersalzberg, Bavaria—even distant. But Martin Jr. tried hard to impress him. When he was eight, he ran to the head of Germany, shot his little arm into the air, and shouted, "Heil Hitler, mein Führer!"

To his dismay, Martin Jr. felt the sting of his father's hand across his cheek—a slap that left him dizzy. "I'd forgotten that to greet the Führer, you had to say, 'Heil,' not 'Heil Hitler," he recounted. Mistakes with the Führer were forbidden.

In 1939, when Martin Jr. was nine, Hitler came to celebrate Christmas at the Bormann house. He brought two very special gifts for his godson— hand-painted Nazi toy soldiers and a detailed toy gun. Martin Jr. delighted in pretending to shoot the

little army men with the gun—casualties of a war he
did not understand.

Toy soldiers like the ones Martin would have played with

His joyful childhood ended when he was sent to an
elite boarding school on Lake Starnberg as a 10-year-
old. Reichsschule Feldafing was the Nazi Party's
academy, about two hours from Martin Jr.'s childhood
home. It was a place to transform German boys into
storm troopers, so play was replaced with order and
discipline.

Order disappeared when the Allied forces stormed into Bavaria on April 15, 1945. Martin Jr. was no longer an elite Nazi student. He was a 15-year-old in danger. He was told to make his way home. His mother and siblings soon fled to Italy to hide, but Martin Jr. was sick at the time, too sick to travel. When he recovered, he was given false identity papers and left to fend for himself.

While Martin Jr. was lost in the rural countryside, a Catholic farmer offered him shelter and opened his eyes to the sins of his father. He became a Catholic priest and spent the rest of his life trying to do good to counter his father's evil.

DID YOU KNOW?

Martin Bormann Sr. was thought to have escaped Nazi Germany to live out his life in hiding, until a body was found in Germany in 1973. There was evidence that it belonged to Bormann, but the identity wasn't confirmed until Martin Bormann Jr. gave law enforcement a DNA sample in 1998. It was a match, and the mystery was solved.

Helmuth Hübener

Helmuth Hübener, a smart boy with electric-blue eyes, was eight years old when Hitler came to power in 1933. His hometown of Hamburg was buzzing with Nazi police called the Gestapo. Any rule broken was punished.

At first, that didn't worry Helmuth much. He worried his brother might be hurt when he went to war for the Nazis. And he didn't like Hitler's ban of the Boy Scouts in 1935. But as a Mormon—a member of the Church of Jesus Christ of Latter-Day Saints—he was taught to obey the laws, so he did.

Worry faded when his brother came home to visit. And joining the Hitler Youth, a Nazi club for active boys, helped fill the scouting gap. During one of his brother's visits, they shared a radio. Tuning in to any program not broadcast by Germany was illegal, and listening to British radio was punishable by death. But that didn't stop Helmuth.

When Helmuth's brother went back to the war, Helmuth moved the radio to his grandparents' apartment. They went to bed early, so at night he listened to any signal he could find. He discovered forbidden programs broadcast by the British Broadcasting Corporation's Allied reporters in German.

A 1940 ad for British radios

Helmuth was smart, so he listened to both sides of the conflict, and came to believe the BBC was telling the truth. Truth was an important part of Helmuth's religion. At 16, he decided to share the facts he'd discovered.

Helmuth had a job as an apprentice at the Hamburg Social Welfare Authority, so he borrowed a typewriter and wrote anonymous articles about the dishonesty of the Nazis. He revealed that the Allies were stronger than Hitler was claiming. He wrote about the murder

of innocent Jews. And he said Germany was not
better under Hitler's rule—it was worse.

> **"MY FATHER IN HEAVEN KNOWS THAT I HAVE DONE NOTHING WRONG."**
> —Helmuth Hübener

He recruited two Mormon friends—Karl-Heinz
Schnibbe and Rudi Wobbe—to help him pass out the
messages. They were afraid, but they tucked papers
into coat pockets and telephone booths. They even
pinned them on public bulletin boards. Their
rebellion remained a secret until Helmuth made a
fatal mistake.

French prisoners of war were jailed near Hamburg,
and Helmuth thought they deserved to know the
truth, too. He asked a man at work to translate the
text into French, and that man turned Helmuth in to
the Gestapo.

At 17, Helmuth was arrested, and his friends soon
joined him. The work was so well-written, the Nazis
were sure an adult had done it, so they tortured the
boys to find out who it was. When torture failed, the
Nazis realized the boys had done it on their own.

They were tried as adults in the Special People's Court in Berlin in August 1942. Karl was sentenced to 10 years in a German work camp. Rudi was sentenced to five years in the same camp. Helmuth was sentenced to death.

When the judge asked them if they had anything to say, Karl and Rudi were silent. But Helmuth spoke. "I have to die now for no crime at all," he said. "But your turn is next."

On October 27, 1942, Helmuth wrote three

A memorial to Helmuth Hübener

farewell letters and was put to death at Plötzensee Prison. He died with his conscience clear.

DID YOU KNOW?

Plötzensee Prison was established in 1868. It took on its dark reputation after the Nazis executed 3,000 men and boys there during World War II.

Len Chester

When Len Chester, born April 5, 1925, joined the British Royal Navy on March 5, 1939—four months before World War II started—he was just 14 years old. At only four feet, ten inches tall, he was "small enough to be placed in the luggage rack to sleep," as he said. But he had all he needed to be a Bugle Boy.

Bugle Boys played military music for their commanding officers and shipmates. They sounded wake-up calls in the morning. They played "Taps" when a crew member died. They boosted spirits and inspired courage.

Len was willing to work hard to earn his title. He had to master 150 bugle calls, plus the

THE NOTES FROM CHARLIE'S BUGLE RANG OUT CLEAR AND LOUD

An illustration of a Bugle Boy from World War I

drum and the flute. "I could never master the 'First Mess' beating on a drum," he remembered, "so the Bugle Major stood behind me with a bass drum stick and repeatedly beat them out on my shoulders until they sunk in."

After his seven months of training was complete in December 1939, he was assigned to serve on a naval base in Scotland on the HMS *Iron Duke*. The rusty old bucket of bolts, nicknamed the "Tin Duck," had once been the pride of the British Royal Fleet.

Severely damaged in World War I, the ship was retired from the open seas, but still served an important purpose near the Scottish shore during World War II. It was an anti-aircraft ship whose guns shot down enemy planes that came within range until the very end.

> "THERE WERE MEN OUT THERE TRYING TO KILL US AND THEY WERE VERY GOOD AT IT, TOO."
> —Len Chester

After he turned 15, Len Chester nearly died on the *Iron Duke* in 1940. Bugle Boys were musicians, but they were also messengers. As German bombs rained down on the *Iron Duke*, Len was on deck, trying to deliver one.

He inched his way along the starboard deck—the right side of the ship when facing the front. The whine of enemy aircraft diving to fire showers of bullets and bombs terrified him, but he had a job to do. When the bullets came too close, he ducked into one of the ship's gun turrets. "I could have been the youngest boy to die in the Second World War," he said. But his quick thinking saved him.

Len was soon reassigned to serve on dangerous Arctic convoy ships. The group of ships delivered tanks, fighter planes, armored vehicles, fuel, ammunition, and food to the Soviet/Russian allies. Enemy forces worked hard to stop them, by any means possible. Len and his mates battled against bombers, U-boats, and raging icy weather to complete their missions.

He was awarded the Arctic Star Medal for his bravery and courage on the convoys. He also received the Soviet Medal of Ushakov for supplying the Red Army with provisions. And finally, Len earned the right to wear the pale yellow beret for his brave conduct on the Arctic convoys. Why yellow? Blood eventually turns yellow when it's spilled onto snow—a fate Len escaped.

The HMS *Iron Duke*

DID YOU KNOW?

"Boogie Woogie Bugle Boy of Company B" was a catchy tribute to musicians like Len Chester. It's been recorded by dozens of popular singers including the Andrews Sisters, Bette Midler, En Vogue, Marie Osmond, the Von Trapp children, Katy Perry, and Pentatonix.

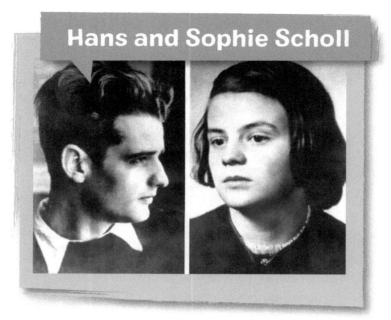

Hans and Sophie Scholl

Hans and Sophie Scholl were freethinking children raised by freethinking parents. And a year after they moved to Ulm, Germany, in 1932, they had a lot to think about: Adolf Hitler was named chancellor on January 30, 1933.

Twelve-year-old Sophie's father, Robert, opposed Hitler's authoritarian ways, but Sophie found the new leader exciting. Hitler promised to restore Germany to a land of strength and wealth. He promised good jobs and plenty to eat. And he said all who followed his strict rules would be happy and free.

Sophie and her four siblings were deceived by Hitler's promises—especially Hans. To his father's dismay, 15-year-old Hans soon joined the Hitler Youth along with thousands of other young German boys. Sophie and her sisters joined the German League of Girls, a club to help train young women to be good Nazi citizens.

For three years, the Scholls tried to be good Germans, but their faith in Hitler soon faded. Sophie loved to read, but her favorite Jewish authors were suddenly forbidden. Hans loved to sing, but some of his favorite songs were banned. Worst of all, they could no longer socialize with their Jewish friends.

A monument to the White Rose, the resistance group Hans and Sophie founded

When those Jewish friends began to disappear, Sophie and Hans were overwhelmed by the injustice. They decided to take action by forming a secret resistance group—a collection of kids who opposed

Hitler's restrictions. At first, they gathered only to sing and talk. But even that got them arrested for disobedience.

Once they were released, their anger was fueled, and it continued to grow. By the time they started classes at the University of Munich, the rebellion had grown bigger and far more determined. They formed a group known as the White Rose to fight Nazi oppression.

The White Rose created essays that disputed hateful Nazi policies. "Every word that comes from Hitler's mouth is a lie," they wrote. "We will not be silent. We are your bad conscience. The White Rose will not leave you in peace."

The Nazi forces were enraged by their actions. Words could be more powerful than guns, and the White Rose generated thousands of them.

When Sophie and Hans carried their last briefcase of flyers to the campus, they scattered them, one stack at a time, throughout a large building. They were cautious, but not cautious enough. A Nazi sympathizer saw them at work, and their fates were sealed.

> **"WHAT DOES MY DEATH MATTER IF,
> BY OUR ACTS, THOUSANDS ARE WARNED
> AND ALERTED?"**
>
> —Sophie Scholl

On February 18, 1943, Hans and Sophie were arrested and charged with treason. Four days later, they were put to death. Hans was just 24 years old. Sophie was 21. The Scholl parents were devastated by the loss, but they were also eternally proud.

DID YOU KNOW?

Sophie and Hans Scholl gave their lives for the sake of truth and justice. But they died for writing only six anti-Nazi leaflets—half a dozen essays that started in Munich and spread across southern Germany. However, roughly 15,000 copies of their pamphlets were distributed, making the White Rose one of the best-known resistance groups of World War II.

Stefania Podgorska

S tefania "Stefi" Podgorska, born June 2, 1923, was a Catholic farm girl living with her family in Lipa, Poland, as Hitler rose to power. But she yearned for the big city of Przemyśl, a few hours away. When her father died in 1939, Stefi's mother gave her permission to move to the city with her sisters. She was 14.

Stefi found a job at the Diamant family's grocery store. The Jewish owner, Mrs. Diamant, was warm and welcoming. Stefi fit right in, especially with one

The city of Przemyśl

of the four Diamant boys, Izidore—Iziu to his friends. They fell in love, but their happiness didn't last.

The Nazis invaded Przemyśl on September 7, 1939, and the Diamant family was forced to move into a Jewish ghetto. They asked Stefi to live in their one-room apartment until they could return. She could see the ghetto from the apartment window.

When Iziu's older brother Max was ordered to go to a Nazi work camp, Iziu took his place. Stefi was heartbroken. She took a train to the camp and bribed a guard to let her speak to Iziu through the fence. He feared for his life, so they hatched a plan. Stefi would return, bribe the guard again, and sneak Iziu home. When the day arrived, Stefi's train was six hours late. By the time she got to the camp, Iziu was dead.

Stefi's mother and brothers were sent to a work camp, too. Her seven-year-old sister, Helena, was hiding with a neighbor in Lipa. Stefi walked four hours to check on her. She was sick, so they walked back to the apartment in Przemyśl together.

Now Stefi had to take care of Helena, but Stefi was only 16, too young to work a real job. The only solution was to pay for forged identity papers that said she was actually 20. With those documents, she landed a job as a machinist making bolts.

Her old friend Max Diamant remained in the Jewish ghetto, haunted by his brother's death. When the Nazis came to send him to a work camp, he hid. But he was discovered and beaten bloody. When he escaped and made his way to his old apartment, Stefi took him in. Others followed.

> **"I DISAGREE THAT PEOPLE CAN KILL OTHER PEOPLE FOR NOTHING. WE ARE ALL PEOPLE AND WE HAVE ONE GOD FOR ALL PEOPLE."**
> —Stefania Podgorska

It was too crowded, so Stefi rented a two-room apartment and secretly moved her friends there. Thirteen Jewish refugees were soon hidden in Stefi's attic. Then the Nazis came knocking.

Nurses at the German hospital across the street needed a place to live. The Nazis wanted Stefi's place, and gave her two hours to pack and leave. She ran through the neighborhood, searching for another apartment, but failed. Her friends begged her to run, but she refused. "I cannot leave you," she told them. She and Helena would stay, no matter what.

When the Nazis returned, they brought miraculous news. Stefi and Helena could stay in one room. The nurses would take the other. For eight months, her

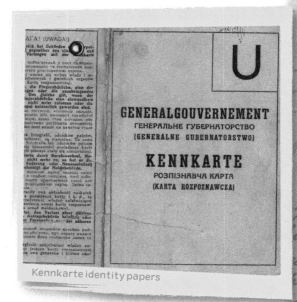

Kennkarte identity papers

13 Jewish friends lived in silence above the Nazi nurses without being discovered.

As the Soviet Allies liberated Przemyśl on July 27, 1944, Max asked Stefi to marry him. She accepted. They lived happily ever after in Israel and America.

DID YOU KNOW?

Nazi identity papers were called *Kennkarte*. Starting in July 1938, all men over 18, all working women over 20, and all Jews were required to carry them.

Adolfo Kaminsky

Adolfo Kaminsky was born in Argentina on October 1, 1925, to a poor family of Russian Jews. They moved to France in 1932, when he was seven, to start a new life. But poverty held them back. Adolfo finished elementary school, then had to give up on his education. He had to find a job to help support his family.

At 15, he was hired at a French clothes-dyeing shop—a place that got color in and out of fabrics. Adolfo learned everything about the tricks of a clothes dyer—how to transform cloth with inks and pigments. He was dazzled by the magic of color and even experimented at home to learn more about it. He became a master—so a better life was within reach.

> "IN ONE HOUR, I MADE 30 FAKE DOCUMENTS. IF I SLEPT FOR ONE HOUR, 30 PEOPLE WOULD DIE."
>
> —Adolfo Kaminsky

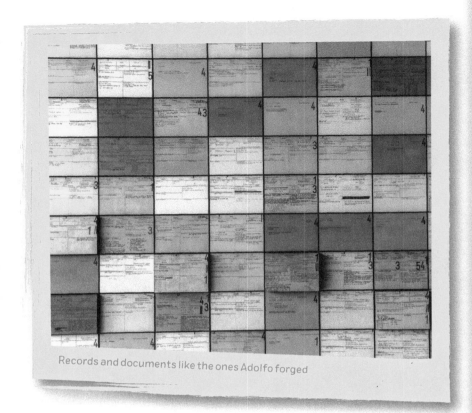

Records and documents like the ones Adolfo forged

But hope was lost when the Nazis invaded France in 1940. Because they were Jewish, Adolfo and his family were driven from their home. This planted a seed of anger in the boy. When the Nazis killed his mother in 1941, the anger blossomed. Adolfo would find a way to fight the Nazi forces, even if he wasn't sure how.

His family was arrested and told they'd be sent to Drancy—a holding place for Jews headed to the death

A memorial to the Jews the Nazis deported in Drancy

camp called Auschwitz. But the family wouldn't give up. Adolfo's brother wrote to the Argentinian government asking for help.

Argentina wanted to remain neutral during the war because many German people lived and vacationed in Argentina. Germany honored the country's choice by treating Argentinians in occupied nations better—people like the Kaminskys.

The Nazis released the Kaminsky family because of their Argentinian travel papers. Adolfo learned an important lesson about official documents that day. But as Jews, they wouldn't escape danger for long. They needed new papers—false ones—to survive. So Adolfo's father paid to have them made, and Adolfo went to make the arrangements.

A man called Penguin met the boy and said he'd call him a student in the new documents. Adolfo said no. "Call me a clothes dyer," he said. Penguin's eyes lit up, and he asked if Adolfo was good with inks. When he answered yes, his anti-Nazi destiny had arrived. Adolfo joined the resistance and began making false documents with Penguin to save lives. He was only 17.

Adolfo and four others rented an apartment to set up a document laboratory. To explain the smell of chemicals drifting out of the space, they told the neighbors they were painters creating art. Then they got to work.

When an order came in for 900 documents in three days, it seemed impossible. But Adolfo refused to sleep. He knew that lives could depend on his efforts, so he met the deadline, though he wasn't quite sure how he did it.

Adolfo spent the rest of the war forging papers to save Jewish people from death camps. It is estimated that Kaminsky saved more than 10,000 children. Even so, he was haunted by those he could not save.

> **DID YOU KNOW?**
>
> Adolfo and his resistance team created travel papers for Jews to escape Nazi-occupied nations, but that wasn't all that they forged. They also created fake food-ration cards, fake birth certificates, fake marriage certificates, and more. They made any documents that might save innocent lives.

Freddie and Truus Oversteegen

"IT WAS TRAGIC AND VERY DIFFICULT AND WE CRIED ABOUT IT AFTERWARDS."

The first thing Freddie Oversteegen lost to Adolf Hitler's war was her bed. She was seven years old and the war hadn't yet come to Haarlem, her hometown in the Netherlands. But waves of desperate refugees were leaving Germany every day in search of a safe place to live.

Haarlem was one of those safe places in the 1930s, so Freddie's mother, Trijn, welcomed them into her floating home—a barge with a spacious cargo hold. Trijn believed in fighting injustice, and that wouldn't change because of the Nazis. So she let homeless Jews, gay people, and others on the run from Hitler stay in the hold. When a weary guest needed a bed,

Freddie had to share the one belonging to her nine-year-old sister, Truus.

The kindness of their mother prepared the Oversteegen girls for their wartime destiny. When the Nazis finally invaded Haarlem in May 1940, Freddie, 14, and Truus, 16, were ready for the fight.

Their parents had divorced by then, so Freddie and Truus now lived with their mother in a small apartment, where they continued to resist the Nazi invaders. At first, they passed out secret messages urging people to fight against the cruel soldiers. With her hair in braids,

The city of Haarlem

Freddie looked about 12—two years younger than she actually was. So when she rode her bicycle past the Nazis, they never questioned what was in her basket.

Eventually, Freddie carried weapons along with the flyers, and still, the soldiers didn't suspect a thing. She was so young and so pretty—how could she be dangerous? It didn't show, but Freddie was very dangerous, and she was about to become even more fierce.

Word of Freddie and Truus's success soon spread among other resistance warriors. Frans van der Wiel, a Haarlem Council of Resistance commander, decided to recruit the teens for more serious missions. Their mother reluctantly gave permission, on one condition. "Always stay human," she told her daughters, and they agreed.

Frans taught the girls how to march and train. He taught them how to sabotage railroads and bridges. And he taught them how to shoot a gun in a dark potato cellar.

Freddie and Truus didn't enjoy the violence. "We did not feel it suited us," Truus said. "It never suits anybody unless they are real criminals." But this was war, and in war people often die.

Even so, the girls had their limits. When the resistance asked the sisters to kidnap the children of a senior Nazi commander, the Oversteegens refused.

"Resistance fighters don't murder children,"
Freddie said.

When the Netherlands were liberated in May 1945, the Oversteegen sisters had survived. They struggled with troubled memories for the rest of their lives, but their kind hearts were intact.

DID YOU KNOW?

Before the Nazis invaded, the Netherlands had been neutral on the war. They felt a closer bond with Germany than they did with Britain. So they were shocked when the Nazis occupied their country. The Netherlands quickly formed an active resistance.

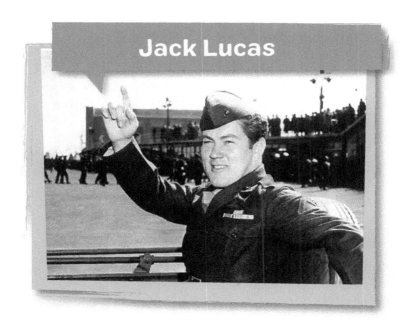

Jack Lucas

hen Jack Lucas, born February 14, 1928, was 11, his father died. Jack was angry and became hard for his mother to handle, so he was sent from his home in North Carolina to the Edwards Military Institute a few hours away. There he found an outlet for his anger: football. Then something knocked his anger up a notch. The Japanese bombed the U.S. Navy's Pearl Harbor military bases in Hawaii on December 7, 1941.

Jack heard about the damage Japan had caused— 188 U.S. aircraft were destroyed, 18 ships were sunk or disabled, 2,403 U.S. soldiers were killed, and

Wreckage of military vehicles at Iwo Jima

1,178 others were wounded. The losses were
overwhelming.

He wanted to help avenge the dead, but he was only
13—four years too young to serve in the U.S. Marine
Corps, even with parental consent. He knew he
would have to wait. But by the time he turned 14 two
months later, Jack's patience was exhausted.

His mother would never sign the paperwork, so he forged her signature and prepared to go to war. How did he convince the marine recruiters he was 17? Jack was really big for his age—five foot eight, 180 pounds, and built like a tank. They never doubted he was old enough.

Jack completed basic training in California and was shipped to Hawaii. When the navy read a letter Jack had written to a friend back home, they discovered he'd lied about his age. So he was only allowed to drive military trucks until his commanding officers could decide what to do with him. Convinced he'd be sent home, he stowed away on a ship.

"I didn't even know where the ships were headed," he said, "but I knew I was on my way to war, and that's what I wanted."

Once the ship was far from land, Jack confessed the truth to his fellow soldiers, but begged to fight with them. Convinced he was ready to serve and unaware of his age, his commanding officers issued Jack a rifle and put him to work. He was about to face the enemy on a Japanese island called Iwo Jima.

The fight was fierce. More than 5,000 U.S. soldiers died in the first two days alone. "Artillery was tearing people up," Jack said. His four-man team made their way to a trench and took cover. His group leader tried to claim the next trench, but it was occupied by 11 Japanese soldiers.

Jack shot two of the men, but then his rifle jammed. He ducked down to clear his gun and saw a Japanese hand grenade at his feet. He screamed, "Grenade!" and threw his body over it to absorb the explosion. Once down, he saw a second grenade. He grabbed it and pulled it under his body, too.

> "I HOLLERED TO MY PALS TO GET OUT AND DID A SUPERMAN DIVE AT THE GRENADES. I WASN'T A SUPERMAN AFTER I GOT HIT."
> —Jack Lucas

Only one went off, but Jack was so badly wounded, his company thought he was dead and left him behind. When a second company arrived, he gave them a sign. "I kept moving the fingers on my left hand to indicate that I was still alive," he said. They rushed him to a field hospital.

Twenty-six surgeries later, Jack was on the mend, but 250 pieces of shrapnel were still embedded in his flesh. He was awarded a chest full of medals, including the Congressional Medal of Honor from President Harry S. Truman. At 17, he was the youngest recipient since the Civil War.

DID YOU KNOW?

Iwo Jima is one of Japan's volcanic islands. When Jack fell on the Japanese grenades, he was able to press them into the soft volcanic ash to help soften the impact of the explosion.

Mariya "Masha" Borisovna Bruskina

For decades, a series of heartbreaking photos appeared in Russian textbooks, films, and museums. Dated October 26, 1941, the first pictures showed a 17-year-old girl with a large wooden sign hanging around her neck. The sign described all the crimes she had committed. It was meant to cause her shame as she was marched through the streets of Minsk, the largest city in the Republic of Belarus.

The next image of "the unknown girl" showed Nazi soldiers slipping a hangman's noose around her neck as she stood on a stool in front of a yeast factory, surrounded by crowds of people. They were watching her sad story unfold.

The Nazis tried to force the teenager to turn and face the audience, but she refused. They tried again, and again—still she denied them. It was as if she was telling her own story—the story of a brave girl resisting German cruelty to the very end.

The girl's death was meant to be a Nazi warning to others who might break the rules. It was to remind them that they could not resist the Germans and survive.

A Russian propaganda poster

Her death had more meaning than the Nazis knew. Her loved ones were afraid to admit they knew her at first, because they feared the Nazis might kill them, too. But in 2009, 68 years after her execution, they finally found the courage to call her by name, and reporters all over the world were ready to listen.

The pictures showed Mariya Borisovna Bruskina—Masha for short. And she was a Jewish heroine; the first Soviet killed resisting the Nazi occupation.

Before the war came to Minsk, Masha, born in 1924, was a good student and a warm, friendly girl. After the war started, she volunteered as a nurse at a Nazi hospital where wounded Soviet soldiers were held. But she had more than medical care in mind.

Masha smuggled civilian clothes and forged travel documents into the hospital so Soviet men could escape their Nazi guards. When she was caught, the Nazis tortured her, but she refused to speak. She died to keep her fellow resistance workers safe.

"IF YOU CAN, PLEASE SEND ME MY DRESS, MY GREEN BLOUSE, AND MY WHITE SOCKS. I WANT TO BE DRESSED DECENTLY WHEN I LEAVE HERE."
—Masha Bruskina

Why did her identity remain a mystery for so long? It's hard to say. Some believe Russian officials were not proud of a Jewish hero. But Masha's uncle didn't believe that. "I can't say we have no anti-Semites," he explained. Anti-Semites are people who are prejudiced against Jews. "Certainly, we have. But they do not rule our lives here."

Whatever the reason, Masha is celebrated now as a freedom fighter who refused to give up, even at the very end. Her story was new to the world, but it was a story the people who knew her best had celebrated all along.

DID YOU KNOW?

The Jewish nation of Israel has honored Masha Bruskina for her courage and determination. A monument was erected in the city of HaKfar HaYarok, and a street was named after her in Jerusalem.

Michael Bornstein

When Israel and Sophie Bornstein brought their second son, Michael, into the world on May 2, 1940, they lived in Żarki, Poland, in a redbrick house with his four-year-old big brother, Samuel.

Żarki had been a happy home for baby Michael and other Jewish families like the Bornsteins. Some parts of Poland denied Jews the right to own property or businesses, but Żarki was different. The town of 3,400 residents offered opportunity to all its people, so more than half of Żarki's citizens were Jews.

Michael's father was an accountant who helped people manage their money. His mother was a stay-at-home mom, and her brother ran a leather tannery. He transformed animal skins into leather for shoes, belts, and handbags.

All of that changed when the Nazis thundered into Poland on Friday, September 1, 1939. The German soldiers murdered 1,000 Jews in a single day—100 in Żarki alone. They also went door-to-door, stealing anything of worth from Jewish families.

Michael's family heard the terrible news from neighbors, so they gathered their valuables—jewelry, fine silver dishes, money—and slipped them

Children at the Auschwitz concentration camp

into a sturdy bag. Then they buried the bag in the backyard for safekeeping. It was the family's first act of resistance.

For five years, the Jews of Żarki lived in danger, never knowing when a Nazi soldier might try to hurt them. Things went from bad to worse. In 1944, Hitler ordered all Jews to be removed from the city.

Michael Bornstein was only four when his family and friends were packed into railroad cattle cars and shipped to a concentration camp called Auschwitz. Once they arrived, his family was separated. His father and brother were sent to the men's side of the camp. Because Michael was so small, he went with his mother and grandmother to the women's **barrack**.

When the guards shaved Michael's curly hair and tattooed his tiny arm, as they did with all prisoners, he was no longer Michael. They called him prisoner B-1148, and he was sent to the children's barrack— away from his mother and grandmother. Only the youngest captives went there, and very few survived.

Sickness was easily spread from child to child, without parents to protect them. Food for small prisoners like Michael was stolen by starving older children. What was left of Michael's hair began to fall out, and he got very weak and thin.

The gates of Auschwitz

Michael's mother tried to help. She snuck into the children's barrack to give him her food. She was beaten for trying to save him, but she didn't care. Again and again, she went back until, finally, she did something even more dangerous. She gathered Michael up and smuggled him back to the women's barrack.

His mother had to work for the Nazis during the daytime, but Michael's grandmother hid him. She was so careful, he remained hidden until the Russian Allies liberated Auschwitz in January 1945. Sadly, his father and brother were killed in the gas chambers four months before the war ended, but his mother and grandmother lived. And Michael was one of the youngest children to survive Auschwitz.

> **"IF WE SURVIVORS REMAIN SILENT . . . THEN THE ONLY VOICES LEFT TO HEAR WILL BE THOSE OF LIARS AND BIGOTS."**
> — Michael Bornstein

When they returned to their old backyard, only one Bornstein treasure was found—a sterling silver kiddush cup used for making blessings. They've cherished the cup as a symbol of faith and survival.

DID YOU KNOW?

Long after World War II ended, Michael Bornstein found his picture on a website that claimed the Holocaust never happened. It made him so angry, he and his daughter wrote a book about his experience to set the record straight.

Calvin Graham, born April 3, 1930, grew up in Crockett, Texas, but he didn't come from a happy home. His stepfather was mean as a snake, so he and his brother moved out when he was only 10 years old. Calvin sold newspapers to pay the bills. He also delivered telegrams on weekends and after school to make ends meet. He didn't see his mother much, but she always stopped by to sign his report cards.

In 1941, when he was 11, the Japanese attacked Hawaii's Pearl Harbor. Calvin was furious. "I didn't like Hitler to start with," he said. But when he discovered some of his cousins had died in the battle, his mind was made up. Calvin wanted to fight.

Unfortunately, at 11, he was too young. So he started to shave in order to thicken his beard, and he waited a year. Then he forged his mother's signature from his report cards and told her he was off to visit relatives. Dressed in his older brother's clothes, complete with a sharp fedora hat, he headed for the recruitment office.

At 12, Calvin was small, just five foot two and 125 pounds. He didn't look 17, so he lined up with other underage boys and waited. The doctor approved them all, but Calvin was worried about the dentist. Teeth don't lie. They reveal your true age.

The crew of the USS *South Dakota*

One by one, the dentist approved the other boys, but he stopped Calvin. Calvin didn't argue. Instead, he asked the dentist why he had approved the other boys but refused him. The dentist changed his mind and approved Calvin, too. "We were losing the war then," Calvin wrote, "so they took six of us."

Calvin was in the U.S. Navy. He completed basic training and boarded the USS *South Dakota*. He quietly turned 13 as they throttled though the Pacific Ocean with a group of other warships on their way to the battle for Guadalcanal in the South Pacific islands.

Eight Japanese destroyers met the U.S. ships head-on. Fire from the *South Dakota* crippled three of them. But when a Japanese searchlight caught them in its beam, the *South Dakota* took 42 direct hits. Calvin was on his gun turret when shrapnel tore through his mouth and jaw, knocking out his front teeth.

> **"I DIDN'T DO ANY COMPLAINING BECAUSE HALF THE SHIP WAS DEAD."**
>
> —Calvin Graham

Dazed and bleeding, Calvin ignored his own injuries and rushed to help other wounded sailors. "I took belts off the dead and made **tourniquets** for the living," he said. When the dust had cleared, 38 men were dead and 60 were wounded.

Calvin was awarded the Purple Heart for being wounded and the Bronze Star for courage in battle. His face was splashed all over naval news reports, along with those of the rest of his crew. His mother spotted him there. She revealed Calvin's true age, so he was jailed, dishonorably discharged, and stripped of his medals and medical benefits. Apart from the scars on his face, it was as if he'd never gone to war.

After years of writing letters to American politicians, Calvin was granted an honorable discharge in 1978. His Bronze Star was returned in 1978. And his disability and medical benefits were restored in 1988. His Purple Heart was finally returned to his family, but only after he had passed away in 1992.

DID YOU KNOW?

The USS *South Dakota* was nearly destroyed in a battle before Calvin came on board. Once it was repaired, the navy radio operators called it *Battleship X* to keep the Japanese from knowing it had survived.

Knud Pedersen

Fourteen-year-old Knud Pedersen was eating breakfast on the morning of April 9, 1940, when he heard the sound of low-flying German planes rumbling above his home in Odense, Denmark. When he ran outside, a flutter of papers drifted down into his yard. The flyers said the Nazis had come to protect the Danish people from the British armies. But they had really come to take over the country.

Knud—who loved art more than politics—grew angry at the thought of Nazi rule. So did his brother Jens and their father, a minister. But most people ignored the danger and went on with their lives. Those people were soon called Hitler's "tame canaries"—creatures happily caged. So Knud and Jens—and a group of cousins and trusted friends from school—formed the RAF Club, named for the Royal Air Force in Great Britain.

One of their first acts of resistance was to destroy newly painted German signs that now hung in the city. Knud and his team had no guns. "We wouldn't

Members of the Churchill Club

have known how to use them, even if we were armed to the teeth," he wrote. So they used what they had: their bicycles.

After the German guards left, two boys would launch their bikes at full speed and crash into the wooden signs. They shattered what they could and redirected what they couldn't, so all the arrows pointed in the wrong directions.

The boys tagged neighborhood walls with anti-swastika symbols. They even cut Nazi telephone lines with garden tools. "And we were doing these things in broad daylight, right after school," Knud said. They had to be home in time for dinner.

Sir Winston Churchill

Soon there were Danish police on every corner of Odense, under Nazi command. They were determined to catch Knud and his club members. But the club was about to disband. Knud and Jens had to move to a new town, and they took the RAF Club name with them. Knud and his brother formed the Churchill Club. The family resistance was stronger than ever, now in two cities instead of one.

"OURS WAS A WAR WITHOUT FRONTS.
MEANING THE ENEMY WAS 360 DEGREES
AROUND US AT ALL TIMES."
—Knud Pedersen

The Churchill Club members grew more careful, but more aggressive. They went from shattering wooden signs to blowing up railroad cars—one filled with Nazi airplane wings. It would be hard to drop bombs from airplanes without wings, the kids thought. That was a great club victory.

Eventually, the Nazis tracked the boys down and put them in jail. But the clever young men slipped in and out of prison under the cover of darkness to continue their missions. They even stole weapons out of Nazis' coat pockets to deliver to the growing anti-Nazi forces.

When Denmark was finally liberated, the Churchill Club members had survived. And in the autumn of 1950, Knud met the club's namesake: Sir Winston Churchill. "Our eyes met for a moment," Knud said. "I felt like I was looking into the devilish eyes of a confidant"—meaning a man who understood him.

DID YOU KNOW?

In 1965, a park in Copenhagen, Denmark, was renamed Churchillparken, in honor of Sir Winston Churchill and the British assistance in freeing the country from Nazi occupation.

Peter MacDonald

When 15-year-old Peter MacDonald saw his cousin's sharp blue uniform in 1944, he made up his mind. He wanted to enlist in the United States Marine Corps to get one of his own. But he was two years too young to sign up, even with his parents' permission.

Then he started thinking. His parents had always told him he was born in 1929, but he didn't know that for sure. He didn't even know what month or day he

Navajo code talkers

had come into the world. On his Navajo Nation reservation, Native children weren't given birth certificates.

The story he'd been told was pretty simple. He was in his mother's belly when they'd started to move their Arizona sheep herd from the winter grazing fields to the summer fields and she'd gone into labor. His father had pitched a tent, laid a soft sheepskin on the ground inside it, and welcomed Peter into the world.

So Peter decided to take a chance and talk to the marine recruiters. He told the story of his birth, except for the part about being born in 1929. Instead, he said he didn't have a birth certificate, but he thought he was 18. To his amazement, the recruiters believed him.

He was bused to San Diego, California, for basic training. As he was walked across the base for a tour, he heard something familiar . . . the sound of Navajo songs floating through the air. He soon met a crew of 28 more Navajo recruits and learned that they would all be part of a very special World War II mission.

The Japanese had broken every code the United States tried to use to send secret battle plans over their radio waves. So the U.S. military gathered a team of Navajo soldiers to try something new. Using their native language, the code talkers would create a new code the Japanese could not break.

> "IF I WAS BY MYSELF, I DON'T KNOW IF I WOULD HAVE MADE IT. BUT I WAS ALWAYS TALKING NAVAJO WITH THESE GUYS."
> —Peter MacDonald

For three months, the Navajo soldiers worked to write and rewrite the new code, based on Navajo word choices, starting with a new version of the American alphabet. "Let's call the letter 'A' bilaSáana," Peter explained. "Bilaśáana in Navajo means 'apple.'" They picked a Navajo word for every letter, "all the way down to 'Z,'" he continued. "Besh-do-tliz, which means 'zinc.'"

In addition to three different versions of the alphabet, they used Navajo words to replace words often used in military messages. "Submarine—besh-lo," Peter said. "Besh-lo in Navajo means 'iron fish.'" By the end of World War II, code talkers like Peter had created and memorized more than 400 words, and they found the courage to remember them even in dangerous conditions.

A memorial to the Navajo code talkers

Peter was one of the youngest code talkers to serve his country. He survived his time in the Marine Corps and went on to be the elected leader of his Navajo Nation—a hero to his community and the whole country.

DID YOU KNOW?

Navajo is the most widely spoken Native American language in the United States. Almost 170,000 American citizens speak Navajo in their homes.

Zinaida Portnova

Zinaida Portnova, born February 20, 1926, was 15 and living with her grandmother and her seven-year-old sister, Galya, when the Nazis rolled into the Soviet Union, now known as Russia. Within a few months, more than 2.5 million Red Army troops fighting for Russia had been killed by the German forces.

When the invaders came to Zui, her grandmother's rural village in Belarus, they were taking anything they wanted, and they wanted her cattle. Most people waited to complain until after the Nazis had left their homes, but Zinaida's grandmother spoke her mind on the spot. Angered by her courage, one Nazi struck the old woman and created a much stronger enemy: Zinaida.

> "WE ARE NOW IN A PARTISAN DETACHMENT . . .
> WE WILL DEFEAT THE NAZI INVADERS."
> —Zinaida Portnova

The teenager's destiny was set on that day in 1941. Zinaida joined a resistance group known as the All-Union Leninist Young Communist League—but most Russians called them the Young Avengers. At 16, she was passing out leaflets and spying on the German forces. She soon moved up to stealing enemy weapons. And once she could handle a gun of her own, she took on sabotage, bombing power plants and factories.

Zinaida had many anti-Nazi victories, but in August 1943, she took on her most dangerous mission. She went undercover in a Nazi **garrison**, posing as cook. Once she was accepted, she took a huge risk: she laced the food with poison.

When Nazi soldiers got sick, and some even died, they suspected Zinaida because she was not German. They questioned her for what must have seemed like hours. She denied it all and volunteered to eat the same food they claimed she had poisoned. When she did not become ill, the Nazis let her leave.

Once the teenager was safely home, she collapsed. Her grandmother fed her bowl after bowl of whey—a watery byproduct of curdled milk. The old woman believed the whey would save her from the poison, and it did. But Zinaida was too weak to go back to work as a cook. When she didn't show up, the Nazis were convinced she was guilty after all.

For a time, the teenager hid in another Russian town. But when she went back home to spy on the Nazis who were searching for her, she was arrested by the Gestapo and jailed. She knew her only hope was to escape. So when one of the German police slammed his pistol on the desk as he questioned her, she took her chance. Zinaida grabbed the gun and killed the Nazi.

A stamp honoring the Young Communist League

As she ran through the forest to the banks of the river Sozh, she was captured and executed by the Nazis. She was just one month away from her 18th birthday when she died, but her legend lives on.

Giuseppe "Pino" Lella

Italian 16-year-old Giuseppe "Pino" Lella, born June 1, 1926, loved clothes and sports and American movies. The town of Milan where he lived had a theater that played those films, so he and his brother, Mimmo, went as often as they could.

World War II hardly touched Pino's family—at first. He lived a beautiful life, even with a dictator like Benito Mussolini running his country. Mussolini wanted to restore the Roman Empire, and he thought joining forces with Hitler would make that easier. But he cared more for power than he did for the people.

Hitler and Mussolini in Berlin

The poor suffered under Mussolini's harsh rule, but people like Pino hardly noticed. While some were begging for scraps, Pino was vacationing at Casa Alpina in the Italian Alps, under the care of a priest named Father Re. "I was always in the mountains," he said. "That's where many people went, out of the city to be at peace."

For three months a year, he enjoyed that natural peace. When the weather was warm, he hiked the difficult mountain trails. When the snow fell, he perfected his skiing. Every day, he grew mentally and physically stronger.

His peace ended in the summer of 1943, when Pino and his brother went to see an American movie called *You Were Never Lovelier,* starring Fred Astaire and Rita Hayworth. He didn't hear the British aircraft flying over Milan at first. But he was confused when the picture on the screen froze and the theater went quiet.

The sound of sirens caused panic and the moviegoers ran for the doors, including Pino and his brother. "We were lucky enough to be among the first to make it out into the open," Pino said. As they cleared the buildings, British bombs hit the back walls of the theater, which came crashing down in a fiery explosion.

The aftermath of the bombing of Milan

A piece of shrapnel cut Pino's cheek, but he wiped the blood away and headed for the safety of his home. With all of Milan's electricity wiped out by the bombs, the only light to guide them came from the city's burning buildings.

> **"I DID NOT WANT TO TALK ABOUT THE WAR. I SAW THINGS THAT I DID NOT WANT TO BE INVOLVED IN."**
> —Giuseppe "Pino" Lella

Knowing how close their children had come to being killed, Pino's parents sent him, Mimmo, and their sister, Francesca, back to Father Re and Casa

Alpina for safety. When the Nazis started sending Italy's Jews to concentration camps to be killed, Father Re turned to Pino for help. The strong boy who loved the mountains so much guided many small groups of seven or eight Jews through the mountain trails to safety in Switzerland.

When Pino turned 18, he had to enlist in the military, so he decided to join the Nazi forces to act as a spy. Because he could speak Italian, German, and French, he was assigned to be a driver for a Nazi officer. Whenever he heard top secret information, he passed it along to the Allies.

Pino survived the war, but he never saw himself as a hero. If fact, when a writer asked to tell his story, he was embarrassed by the offer.

DID YOU KNOW?

Mark Sullivan wrote a book about Pino's life called *Beneath a Scarlet Sky*, which will be made into a television miniseries. *Spider-Man* actor Tom Holland will play Pino. That news made the real Pino smile.

Bill Edwardes

When Bill Edwardes, born November 7, 1926, was 14, he left school to work in a **munitions** factory in London, England. World War II had started the year before, and making bombs, shells, and cartridges for battle made him feel like he was part of the fight. Two years later, he took a bolder step and actually joined the army, lying about his age since he was not allowed to join until he was 18 years old.

At 16, Bill was too young to enlist, so he told the recruiting sergeant he was 17½. Though he was small, the officer believed him, and he was assigned to the First **Battalion** of the Worcestershire Regiment as an infantryman. Dressed in his uniform, he felt proud.

Trouble was, since he was only 16 and so small, he was sent to a camp for undersized soldiers, where he suffered a terrible injury. He feared his military career was over until his sergeant called for three volunteers. Bill's hand shot up, and his fate was decided. "Right!" his sergeant said. "You will be a stretcher-bearer."

Stretcher-bearers were part of the medical team in the British Army. Bill spent six weeks learning how to care for wounded soldiers. He carried a medical pack with medicine and a special ID that proved he was noncombative—he was on the battlefield to save lives, not take them. Under the Geneva Convention, the international rules of war, noncombatants were protected. But the Nazis cared nothing for the rules of war. They targeted stretcher-bearers on purpose.

Stretcher-bearers carrying a wounded soldier

The job was dangerous, but Bill was being trained well. He learned how to check the patient's breathing and to recognize blood loss. He learned how to splint

The invasion of Normandy

broken bones and to bandage wounds. And he learned how to give the painkiller morphine.

Once his training was complete, Bill faced the ultimate challenge. He would be a part of the Normandy invasion against German troops in France. He would help launch D-Day. On June 6, 1944, 24,000 British, American, and Canadian soldiers would storm the beaches in amphibious transports launched from ships. Even more soldiers would join the battle by air.

> "I WAS 12 WHEN WAR BROKE OUT. I WA~~S~~
> WHEN IT ENDED. PEOPLE SAY TO ME, "~~
> WAS YOUR YOUTH GONE.' BUT IT DIDN'T Go~~.
> IT WAS JUST SPENT IN A DIFFERENT WAY.
> I WAS SAVING PEOPLE'S LIVES."

—Bill Edwardes

German casualties were high—as many as 9,000 men—but Allied deaths were higher—at least 10,000. It was Bill's job to treat and comfort the wounded. "There was me," he wrote, "a 17-year-old boy, cradling these senior officers, men in their late 20s or their 30s, holding them in my arms, looking after them."

The risk was enormous, but young Bill survived every battle.

DID YOU KNOW?

During World War II, British troops were not allowed to stop and rescue their wounded. Instead, each soldier carried an emergency medical kit to treat their own wounds long enough to wait for their unit stretcher-bearers. Each company of men had only four stretcher-bearers, so the wait was sometimes a long one.

Sergey Aleshkov

T oward the end of World War II, thousands of very young children had been orphaned or abandoned all over Eastern Europe. Without families to care for them, they depended on luck and the kindness of strangers.

In time, those children became known as the "wolf children"—children forced to survive alone in the wild. When the Nazis rolled into his village in the Kaluga region of Russia in 1942, six-year-old Sergey Aleshkov became one of those lost, lonely children.

The Germans were in search of partisans, people fighting in secret to rid the world of Nazis. Sergey's 10-year-old brother, Petya, was accused of that crime. Though his mother begged for mercy, she and Petya were both killed.

Sergey would have been shot, too, but a neighbor scooped him up, carried him to her back window, pushed him out, and told him to run. Terrified, Sergey followed her instructions. He ran, but where could he go? He had nothing and no one.

When Red Army scouts found him wandering through the woods, he was tired, dirty, and covered in cuts and insect bites. He had no birth certificate and no memory of when he was born. His rescuers could only guess at his age, and they guessed six.

Russian soldiers during World War II

They wrapped him in a horse blanket and took him to their commanding officer, a Soviet Marshal named Mikhail Vorobyev. Sergey could remember his full name, but when they asked about his mother, he broke into tears. The marshal assumed she was gone, so he made a decision. Sergey would stay with him and the 47th Guards Rifle Division.

Russian civilians migrating after the German invasion

The little boy got the medical care he needed, a tiny uniform, and a brand-new father in Mikhail Vorobyev, who had no wife or children of his own.

The division found jobs for Sergey. He was a special assistant to his father. He carried messages across the base. He delivered incoming mail and newspapers. During more dangerous moments, Sergey passed out cups of water and ammunition.

If anyone doubted Sergey's value, their minds were changed when he noticed a group of strangers hiding behind a haystack. He told his father, and the troops investigated and found that they were German spies. When his father was trapped under falling bricks and wood after an explosive landed in the base, Sergey ran for help and saved him. For his bravery, he won the Medal "For Battle Merit" and a pistol of his own.

When his father met a nurse named Nina Bedova, he fell in love with her, and they were married. When the war ended, they went to Sergey's old village to be sure he didn't have family waiting for him. There was no one left, but Sergey lived happily with his new parents in the quiet Russian town of Chelyabinsk.

DID YOU KNOW?

There are no records, but some historians believe there were thousands of wolf children in Russia after the war. Most were German, the children of the enemy, so they had trouble finding help. In time, farmers adopted some of the younger orphans and offered jobs to those old enough to work. But experts agree that many wolf children did not survive.

Kiku Nakayama

K iku Nakayama was born on Okinawa Island on December 5, 1929—the anniversary of Emperor Hirohito's first day on the Japanese throne. In celebration of the emperor, she was given the name Kiku. "Kiku" means "chrysanthemum," a flower that is a vibrant symbol of the royal family.

For 16 years, Kiku lived a traditional Japanese life. Then World War II came to her island home. Hitler was about to surrender to Allied forces in Europe, so the American forces focused on Japan. They wanted

American troops in Okinawa

to control Okinawa Island because its Kadena Air Base would be the perfect place to launch an attack on the bigger Japanese islands.

The attack was soon known as the Typhoon of Steel, and it was long and ferocious. From April 1, 1945, to June 22, 1945, the Allied forces attacked Okinawa by air, sea, and land. More than 200,000 people died in the battle for the southern Japanese island. Half of them were civilians.

American planes conducting an air strike on Okinawa

Kiku had become a volunteer nurse for the Imperial Army one month before the Americans landed, along with 55 other girls from the Daini Girls High School, where she was enrolled. What started as a public-service project turned into a horrible nightmare in a matter of weeks.

Because the losses were so great, the hospital quickly ran out of medical supplies. Kiku and the other teenage nurses were forced to help doctors perform surgeries without **anesthesia** to numb the pain. They hopelessly reassured dying men when they knew many would not survive. And when the nurses could no longer care for the wounded, they were told to find their own way home through the violent war zone.

Before they left, the girls were told the American soldiers would torture them, or worse. To protect them from that fate, the troops gave each nurse two grenades—one to throw at the enemy, and one to take their own lives. They said the explosives were "benevolent gifts from the emperor," and wished the girls luck.

> "I THOUGHT I'D BE BETTER OFF DEAD. BUT I WAS TOO SCARED TO USE A GRENADE."
> —Kiku Nakayama

As she struggled to make her way through a rainstorm of bombs and shells, Kiku saw death all around her, but she felt nothing. Hope had left her, so she considered using one of her grenades. But when a friend refused to take her own life, Kiku decided against it, too.

Kiku was captured by American soldiers and held for about 10 days, but not for torture. She was held for her own safety, until the fighting had ended. But 22 of the student nurses had been killed in the battle. Even now, more than 75 years later, Kiku feels guilty about not dying with them. "Every day," Kiku said, "I wonder why I survived and not them." And every day, she prays the world will never again experience a war like the one she survived.

DID YOU KNOW?

In 2007, Japan's Prime Minister Shinzō Abe decided to change the country's school history books. He wanted to erase all mention of Japan's wartime practice of suicide. Kiku Nakayama was shocked. It was her truth they wanted to forget, and she did not approve. So she joined 100,000 people in Tokyo to protest the change. Abe still altered the written history, but Kiku will keep the truth alive as long as she is able to.

Junko Kayashige

In August 1945, Junko Kayashige was a six-year-old living in Hiroshima, Japan, with her parents, one brother, and six sisters. She had started elementary school four months earlier, but rumors of American bombs sent her family to the countryside. It was a safer place to learn.

Summer break brought them back to the city of 350,000 citizens. Junko's brother joined the Japanese Imperial Army and was training far from Hiroshima. The rest of her family was home and busy.

On August 6, Junko's mother gathered up her baby sister and announced that she was going to visit a sick relative. Junko's older sisters would babysit. Another sister, Michiko, begged to go, but her mother refused. Michiko had just learned to ride a bicycle, so she decided to ride to the store to get ice. Another sister, Hiroku, was gone. She was helping to build a firebreak to protect the city, in case more American bombs fell.

Bored, Junko and her little sister Fumie walked to their uncle's house. Junko loved to visit him because he put on music so the little girls could dance. As they twirled around the living room, Junko spied an airplane in the sky. She and her cousin ran to the big glass window to get a better look.

"It's a B-29," Junko called out, tracking an American plane called the Enola Gay. The six-year-old had no sense of the destruction about to hit Hiroshima. But the bomber would drop a 9,000-pound atomic bomb nicknamed Little Boy. And Junko was about to survive the first nuclear bombs ever used in combat.

The nuclear bomb exploding in Hiroshima

With a blistering heat that rivaled the sun, the bomb exploded 1,800 feet above Hiroshima. 100,000 people were killed in a flash. Junko and her cousin were knocked from the window, unconscious

The aftermath of the bombing of Hiroshima

on her uncle's living room floor. When she came to, the world had become a dark, confusing place.

Junko's aunt, uncle, and little sister were blown into another room. Their furniture was in splinters. The house didn't crumble, but many others did. Junko went outside. Everything was on fire, so she panicked and ran. Another relative caught her and took her to her mother.

Junko's father searched for his missing children. Hiroku was so badly burned, he hardly recognized her when he found her at a nearby school. She'd been tying her shoe when the bomb exploded, so the wounds on her back were especially brutal. Hiroku fought for 10 days to survive, then passed away from her nuclear burns. Michiko—who had gone for ice on her bicycle before the bomb fell—was never found.

> **"I WANTED TO DEPICT THE FOOLISHNESS OF HUMANS WHO ATTEMPT TO SOLVE PROBLEMS WITH WAR AND DESTRUCTION."**
> —Junko Kayashige, on her art

Junko lost two sisters to Hiroshima's nuclear horrors, and she spent the rest of her life telling her story and creating powerful artwork, which she hoped would help prevent more wars. She could not change the past, but she had hope for the future.

DID YOU KNOW?

Between 90,000 and 146,000 people died after the atomic bomb dropped on Hiroshima, Japan. Three days later, a second atomic bomb fell on Nagasaki and killed between 39,000 and 80,000 Japanese people, mostly civilians.

GLOSSARY

amphibious: Suited for both land and water

anesthesia: Injection or breathable gas to temporarily block pain during a medical procedure

annex: An extension added to a building for extra space

anonymous: Unidentified, unknown

artillery: Large guns, cannons, or missiles

authoritarian: A person who demands strict obedience at the expense of others' freedom

barrack: A building for lodging soldiers or prisoners

battalion: A large group of military troops ready for battle

Catholic: One branch of the Christian religious belief system

domination: Complete control over other people

extermination: The killing of living things, usually in mass numbers

forged: Illegally produced copies of documents like passports

führer: A leader who is willing to take power at any cost, for his own benefit; Hitler's title as head of Nazi Germany

garrison: Troops in place to defend a town or fortress

Gestapo: The Nazis' secret police

ghetto: A part of a city where minority groups of people are forced to live

grenade: A small missile containing an explosive or harmful chemical

ideology: A system of beliefs adopted by groups

machinist: A person who builds or fixes a machine or tool

Mormon: A member of the Church of Jesus Christ of Latter-Day Saints, a branch of Christianity

munitions: Weapons, including guns, bombs, and other equipment, used in a war

Nazi: A member of the National Socialist German Workers' Party, formed by Adolf Hitler

oppression: Prolonged, unjust treatment and control

partisan: Belonging to a group or a cause

pigments: Natural coloring elements used for paints and cloth

politician: A person who is professionally involved in government

rebellion: Refusing to obey a ruler or government's unfair rules

refugee: A person forced to leave their home to escape injustice or war

resistance: The act of refusing to obey rules one believes are unjust

restitution: Repaying the cost of things damaged or caused to be damaged

Romany: A group of often mistreated Eastern European people once known as Gypsies

sabotage: To damage a place or property on purpose to cause trouble

shrapnel: Metal pieces of a bomb launched by an explosion

technology: Science used to solve modern problems

tourniquet: A device used to stop blood loss from a wound

treaties: Official written agreements between countries

trench: A narrow ditch dug by soldiers to provide a safer place to do battle

RESOURCES

BOOKS

Remember World War II: Kids Who Survived Tell Their Stories by Dorinda Nicholson. National Geographic, 2005.

Surviving Hitler: A Boy in the Nazi Death Camps by Andrea Warren. HarperCollins, 2002.

World War II for Kids: A History with 21 Activities by Richard Panchyk. Chicago Review Press, 2002.

World War II: The Definitive Visual History from Blitzkrieg to the Atom Bomb. DK Publishing, 2015.

World War II: Visual Encyclopedia. DK Children, 2015.

MUSEUMS

National World War II Museum
    945 Magazine Street
    New Orleans, LA 70130
    NationalWW2Museum.org

Smithsonian National Museum of American History
    1300 Constitution Avenue NW
    Washington, DC 20560
    AmericanHistory.si.edu

United States Holocaust Memorial Museum
100 Raoul Wallenberg Place SW
Washington, DC 20024
USHMM.org

WEBSITES

Anne Frank (House and Museum)
AnneFrank.org/en

National World War II Museum
NationalWW2Museum.org

National World War I Museum and Memorial
TheWorldWar.org

United States Holocaust Memorial Museum
USHMM.org

REFERENCES

BOOKS

Alexievich, Svetlana. *Last Witnesses: An Oral History of the Children of World War II.* New York: Modern Library, 2020.

Bornstein, Michael, and Debbie Borstein Holinstat. *Survivors Club: The True Story of a Very Young Prisoner of Auschwitz.* New York: Square Fish, 2019.

Chester, Len. *Bugle Boy.* Ebrington: Long Barn Books, 2007.

Dumbach, Annette and Jud Newborn. *Sophie Scholl and the White Rose.* London: Oneworld Publications, 2018.

Frank, Anne. *The Diary of a Young Girl.* New York: Bantam, 1993.

Hoose, Phillip M. *The Boys Who Challenged Hitler: Knud Pedersen and the Churchill Club.* New York: Square Fish, 2019.

Macadam, Heather Dune. *999: The Extraordinary Young Women of the First Official Jewish Transport to Auschwitz.* New York: Citadel Press, 2020.

Tucker, Spencer C. *Encyclopedia of World War II: A Political, Social, and Military History.* Santa Barbara: ABC-Clio, 2006.

ARTICLES

BBC. "History: World War Two." 2014. bbc.co.uk/history/worldwars/wwtwo.

Blakemore, Erin. "Meet the Youngest Person Executed for Defying the Nazis." *History.* Last modified August 31, 2018. history.com/news/meet-the-youngest-person-executed-for-defying-the-nazis.

———. "The Secret Student Group That Stood Up to the Nazis." *Smithsonian Magazine.* February 22, 2017. smithsonianmag.com/smart-news/the-secret-student-group-stood-up-nazis-180962250/.

Burns, Lucy. "White Rose: The Germans Who Tried to Topple Hitler." *BBC News.* February 22, 2013. bbc.com/news/magazine-21521060.

Chester, Len. "WW2 People's War Funerals." BBC.co.uk. April 6, 2004. bbc.co.uk/history/ww2peopleswar/stories/80/a2497980.shtml.

Distasio, Jim. "WW II Freedom Fighter Pino Lella." *Fra Noi*. March 31, 2018. franoi.com/profiles/ww-ii-freedom-fighter-pino-lella.

Druckerman, Pamela. "'If I Sleep for an Hour, 30 People Will Die.'" *New York Times*. October 2, 2016. nytimes.com/2016/10/02/opinion /sunday/if-i-sleep-for-an-hour-30-people-will-die.html.

Farmer, Brit McCandless. "The Forger Who Saved Thousands of Jews from the Nazis." *CBS News*. October 29, 2017. cbsnews.com/news /the-forger-who-saved-thousands-of-jews-from-the-nazis.

Fink, Jenni. "National Purple Heart Day: Youngest Recipient, Calvin Graham, Was Only 13 Years Old." *Newsweek*. August 7, 2018. newsweek.com/national-purple-heart-day-youngest-recipient -was-only-13-years-old-1059491.

Fletcher, Gail, and Lukas Kreibig. "The Forgotten 'Wolf Children' of World War II." *National Geographic*. July 29, 2019. nationalgeographic.com/culture/2019/07/forgotten-wolf -children-world-war-ii.

Fukuda, Masanori. "Wartime Okinawa Student Nurse Recalls Terror of Battle, Urges Youth to Resist Militarism." *Japan Times*. May 22, 2015. japantimes.co.jp/news/2015/05/22/national/history /wartime-okinawa-student-nurse-recalls-terror-battle-urges -youth-resist-militarism/#.XhZbwMhKg2w.

Gauvin, Jean-Baptiste. "Adolfo Kaminsky: The Photographer Forger." *Blind*. August 20, 2019. blind-magazine.com/en/news/612 /Adolfo-Kaminsky-The-Photographer-Forger.

German Resistance Memorial Center. "Helmuth Hübener." gdw-berlin.de/en/recess/biographies/index_of_persons/biographie /view-bio/helmuth-huebener/?no_cache=1.

Getlen, Larry. "How Nazi Offspring Dealt with Their Families' Hellish Histories." *New York Post*. February 3, 2018. nypost.com/2018/02 /03/how-nazi-offspring-dealt-with-their-familys-hellish-histories.

Haberman, Clyde. "A Quiet Visitor to Israel: Martin Bormann's Son." *New York Times*. April 21, 1993. nytimes.com/1993/04/21/world /a-quiet-visitor-to-israel-martin-bormann-s-son.html.

Hatherley, Sam. "Tributes to Veteran Bill Who Took Part in D-Day Landings Aged Just 17." *Hampshire Chronicle.* May 22, 2019. hampshirechronicle.co.uk/news/17657653.tributes-to-veteran -bill-who-took-part-in-d-day-landings-aged-just-17.

HistoryExtra. "The Boys Who Lied about Their Age to Fight in WW2." March 6, 2019. historyextra.com/period/second-world-war/ boys-who-lied-about-age-to-fight-ww2-teenage-soldiers.

Hogg, Chris. "Hiroshima Survivors Keep Memories Alive." *BBC News.* August 3, 2005. news.bbc.co.uk/2/hi/asia-pacific/4735163.stm.

Ishak, Natasha. "Zinaida Portnova: The Teenage Partisan Who Became a Soviet Hero during World War II." *All That's Interesting.* Last modified January 3, 2020. allthatsinteresting.com/zinaida -portnova.

Kataoka, Yuki. "Okinawa Nurse Recalls WWII's Darkest Hour." *Stars & Stripes Japan.* June 12, 2015. japan.stripes.com/community-news /okinawa-nurse-recalls-wwiis-darkest-hour-1547824628.

Katz, Brigit. "Freddie Oversteegen, Teenage Resistance Fighter Who Assassinated Nazis, Has Died at 92." *Smithsonian Magazine.* September 18, 2018. smithsonianmag.com/smart-news/freddie -oversteegen-who-assassinated-nazis-teenage-resistance -fighter-has-died-92-180970319.

Kayashige, Junko. "My Experience of the Atomic Bombing." University of Iowa Archive, lib.uiowa.edu/wwwarchive/eac /HiroshimaNagasaki/Kayashige.pdf.

Keller, Bill. "Echo of '41 in Minsk: Was the Heroine a Jew?" *New York Times.* September 15, 1987. nytimes.com/1987/09/15/world/echo -of-41-in-minsk-was-the-heroine-a-jew.html.

Kennedy, J. Michael. "Sisters Reunited With Jews They Saved From Nazis: World War II: Unlikely Protectors Were Youngsters When They Hid 13 People in a Cramped Polish Apartment." *Los Angeles Times.* January 10, 1995. latimes.com/archives/la-xpm-1995 -01-10-mn-18462-story.html.

King, Gilbert. "The Boy Who Became a World War II Veteran at 13 Years Old." *Smithsonian Magazine.* December 19, 2012. smithsonianmag.com/history/the-boy-who-became-a-world -war-ii-veteran-at-13-years-old-168104583.

Kostro, Zak. "One of the Last Living Holocaust Survivors Shares His Stories From Auschwitz." *Esquire.* April 10, 2017. esquire.com /entertainment/books/a54327/survivors-club-michael-bornstein -debbie-bornstein-holinstat.

Lella, Michael. "My Father's Role in the Fall of Fascism: The True Story behind the 2017 Bestseller *Beneath a Scarlet Sky.*" Foundation for Economic Education. May 3, 2018. fee.org/articles/my-fathers-role -in-the-fall-of-fascism.

Lisciotto, Carmelo. "Sophie Scholl." Holocaust Education & Archive Research Team. 2007. holocaustresearchproject.org/revolt /scholl.html.

Little, Becky. "This Teenager Killed Nazis with Her Sister during WWII." *History.* Last modified March 1, 2019. history.com/news /dutch-resistance-teenager-killed-nazis-freddie-oversteegen.

Milam, Whitney. "Sophie Scholl: The German Student Who Led an Anti-Nazi Resistance Movement." *Medium:* Amy Poehler's Smart Girls. April 2, 2017. amysmartgirls.com/sophie-scholl-the -german-student-who-led-an-anti-nazi-resistance-movement -ef4c8d2f4d96.

Moore, Matthew. "Pino Lella: Hollywood to Tell the Story of Wartime Boy Hero Who Rescued Jews from Italy." *Times.* August 29, 2017. thetimes.co.uk/article/hollywood-calls-for-pino-lella-wartime -boy-hero-qwlnz6hdp.

Morales, Laurel. "Navajo Code Talkers: The 'Miracle' That Ended the World's Deadliest War." *Fronteras.* Last modified May 1, 2020. fronterasdesk.org/content/1005301/navajo-code-talkers-miracle -ended-world-war-ii.

Neilsen, Harald. "Anne Frank and Her Family." Holocaust Education & Archive Research Team. 2007. holocaustresearchproject.org/ nazioccupation/annefrank.html.

O'Leary, Naomi. "'Her War Never Stopped': The Dutch Teenager Who Resisted the Nazis." *Guardian.* September 23, 2018. theguardian .com/world/2018/sep/23/freddie-oversteegen-dutch-teenager -who-resisted-nazis.

Pace, Eric. "Calvin Graham, 62, Who Fought in War As a 12-Year-Old." *New York Times.* November 9, 1992. nytimes.com/1992/11/09 /obituaries/calvin-graham-62-who-fought-in-war-as-a-12-year -old.html.

Portsmouth City Council. "The D-Day Story Collection." The D-Day Story, Portsmouth. 2020. theddaystory.com/Search/Detail/4849.

Reynolds, Isabel. "Japan's History Divide Comes Home in Textbook Row." Reuters. October 18, 2007. reuters.com/article/us-japan-war -suicides/japans-history-divide-comes-home-in-textbook-row -idUST896120071019.

Roberts, Sam. "Freddie Oversteegen, Gritty Dutch Resistance Fighter, Dies at 92." *New York Times.* September 25, 2018. nytimes.com /2018/09/25/obituaries/freddie-oversteegen-dutch-resistance -fighter-dies-at-92.html.

Sahouri, Andrea May. "One of the Youngest Holocaust Survivors to Speak in Des Moines, Ames." *Des Moines Register.* September 14, 2019. desmoinesregister.com/story/news/2019/09/14/holocaust -survivor-speak-iowa-des-moines-aimes-auschwitz-michael -bornstein-debbie-holinstat-prisoner/2326905001.

Sanai, Darius. "The Sins of My Father." *Independent.* February 1, 1999. independent.co.uk/arts-entertainment/the-sins-of-my-father -1068013.html.

Scully, Louis. "Wounded in Action (N.W. Europe 1944–45)—1st Battalion Worcestershire Regiment." The Worcestershire Regiment. Last modified 2015. worcestershireregiment.com/wounded_in _action_WW2.php.

Seidel, Jamie. "How 'Innocent' Teen Lured Nazis to Their Deaths." News.com.au. January 19, 2020. news.com.au/lifestyle/real-life /news-life/how-innocent-teen-lured-nazis-to-their-deaths/news -story/49417ffa39298d768cf98fe081f17ccc.

Silvam, Prabhu. "'Worse than Death': The Children Who Survived the Battle for Okinawa." *South China Morning Post.* May 6, 2018. scmp.com/week-asia/society/article/2144267/worse-death -children-who-survived-battle-okinawa.

Silversmith, Shondiin. "For Navajo Code Talker Peter MacDonald, a 'Beautiful Blue' Uniform Led Him to Enlist at 15." *Arizona Republic.* August 29, 2019. azcentral.com/story/news/local/arizona/2019/08/29/navajo-code-talker-peter-macdonald-ww-2-marines/1935106001.

Simkin, John. "Stretcher Bearers." *Spartacus Educational.* Last modified January 2020. spartacus-educational.com/FWWstretcher.htm.

Smith, Harrison. "Freddie Oversteegen, Dutch Resistance Fighter Who Killed Nazis through Seduction, Dies at 92." *Washington Post.* September 16, 2018. washingtonpost.com/local/obituaries/freddie-oversteegen-dutch-resistance-fighter-who-killed-nazis-through-seduction-dies-at-92/2018/09/16/7876eade-b9b7-11e8-a8aa-860695e7f3fc_story.html.

Spanjer, Noor. "This 90-Year-Old Lady Seduced and Killed Nazis as a Teenager." *Vice.* May 11, 2016. vice.com/en_us/article/dp5a8y/teenager-nazi-armed-resistance-netherlands-876.

Stellabotte, Ryan. "Stories Survive: A Child of the Holocaust Reclaims a Resilient Heritage." *Fordham Magazine.* June 30, 2017. news.fordham.edu/fordham-magazine/stories-survive-a-child-of-the-holocaust-reclaims-a-resilient-heritage.

Takada, Yoshinori. "Battle of Okinawa Survivors Speak of Mixed Feelings about the Emperor System, Memories of War, and the Emperor's Visits to Okinawa (Heisei and Okinawa)." *Ryukyu Shimpo.* April 28, 2019. english.ryukyushimpo.jp/2019/05/04/30336/.

Telegraph. "Bill Edwardes BEM, Landed on D-Day Aged 17 to Be a Stretcher Bearer, One of the Most Dangerous Jobs in an Infantry Unit—Obituary." June 5, 2019. telegraph.co.uk/obituaries/2019/06/05/bill-edwardes-landed-d-day-aged-17-stretcher-bearer-one-dangerous.

Telegraph. "Nazi Poster Reveals Execution of Teenager Who Listened to BBC." September 28, 2010. telegraph.co.uk/history/world-war-two/8029845/Nazi-poster-reveals-execution-of-teenager-who-listened-to-BBC.html.

United States Holocaust Memorial Museum. "Stefania (Fusia) Podgorska: ID Card." encyclopedia.ushmm.org/content/en/id-card /stefania-fusia-podgorska.

Vincent, Isabel. "Meet the Dutch Girls Who Seduced Nazis—and Lured Them to Their Deaths." *New York Post.* December 14, 2019. nypost. com/2019/12/14/meet-the-dutch-girls-who-seduced-nazis -and-lured-them-to-their-deaths.

Walsh, Colleen. "Memories of Armageddon." *Harvard Gazette.* October 11, 2011. news.harvard.edu/gazette/story/2011/10 /memories-of-armageddon.

WEBSITES

Anne Frank House. AnneFrank.org.

History. "World War II." A&E Television Networks. Last modified October 1, 2019. history.com/topics/world-war-ii/ world-war-ii-history.

Holocaust Memorial Resource & Education Center of Florida. "June 12, 1942—Anne Frank." HolocaustEdu.org/education/research/ this-week-in-history/june-12-1942-anne-frank.

Miep Gies: Her Own Story. "Declaration of Margot Frank's Death." MiepGies.nl/en/biography/special%20documents/272.html.

The Takeaway. "A Child's Escape from Auschwitz." WNYC Studios. March 8, 2017. WNYCStudios.org/podcasts/takeaway/segments/ surviving-auschwitz-toddler.

VIDEOS

Boy Soldiers of WW2. Directed by Craig Collinson. New York: Ammo Content, 2014. Amazon Prime Video.

Burzminski, Ed. "Ed Burzminski Talk about Stefania Podgorska at Arizona Jewish History Museum May 2019." YouTube video. Posted May 9, 2019. youtube.com/watch?v=1e3YhvSocmQ.

CGTN America. "Full Frame Close Up: Surviving Auschwitz." YouTube video. Posted November 2, 2017. youtube.com/watch ?v=dJitqNbbeS0.

Hitler's Children. Directed by Chanoch Zeevi. New York: Film Movement, 2011. Amazon Prime Video.

Lafayette College. Lafayette President Dan Weiss: The Case of Masha Bruskina. YouTube video. Posted November 20, 2007. youtube.com/watch?v=TkI7hVcOhOY.

MedalOfHonorBook. "Jack Lucas, Medal of Honor, WWII." YouTube video. Posted September 27, 2011. youtube.com /watch?v=_aGhPjeayJY.

New York Times. *The Forger.* YouTube video. Posted October 3, 2016. youtube.com/watch?v=Dup6KOoaAUc.

Rabbit Ears TV. "Truth & Conviction: The Helmuth Hubener Story (Teenage Nazi Resistance Fighter)." YouTube video. Posted July 9, 2017. youtube.com/watch?v=ICswA1YnvA8.

s20hibaku. "A-bomb Victims Voice / Ms. Junko Kayashige – Part 1." YouTube video. Posted March 1, 2010. youtube.com/watch ?v=5CeiWU6G4CU.

———. "A-bomb Victims Voice / Ms. Junko Kayashige – Part 2." YouTube video. Posted March 1, 2010. youtube.com/watch ?v=IUSxdaIgl0A.

———. "A-bomb Victims Voice / Ms. Junko Kayashige – Part 3." YouTube video. Posted March 1, 2010. youtube.com/watch ?v=VxF3TX2dcKk.

The Short Life of Anne Frank. Directed by Gerrit Netten. Amsterdam: Anne Frank House, 2001. annefrank.org/en/education/product /132/video-the-short-life-of-anne-frank/.

University of California Television (UCTV). "Hiroshima Survivors Tell of the First Atomic Attack." YouTube video. Posted May 21, 2009. youtube.com/watch?v=XKlf5VXpYpY.

University of Southern California. "Stefania Podgorska Burzminski on Being a Rescuer." USC Shoah Foundation video. sfi.usc.edu/video /stefania-podgorska-burzminski-being-rescuer.

INDEX

ABOUT THE AUTHOR

 **KELLY MILNER HALLS** has written nonfiction for young readers for almost 25 years. She believes kids are the promise of tomorrow and are worth the best research and writing she can manage. She lives in Spokane, Washington, with two daughters, a Great Dane named Abbey, and too many rescue kitties, but who's counting? For more about her work, visit her website at WondersOfWeird.com.

CPSIA information can be obtained
at www.ICGtesting.com
Printed in the USA
JSHW012045160720
6738JS00004B/19